T0127515

PERFECT TARTS

PERFECT TARTS

20 DELECTABLE RECIPES SHOWN IN 100 PHOTOGRAPHS

MAGGIE MAYHEW

LORENZ BOOKS

This edition is published by Lorenz Books, an imprint of Anness Publishing Ltd,
Blaby Road, Wigston, Leicestershire LE18 4SE; info@anness.com
www.lorenzbooks.com; www.annesspublishing.com

If you like the images in this book and would like to investigate using them for
publishing, promotions or advertising, please visit our website www.practicalpictures.com
for more information.

publisher Joanna Lorenz
managing editor Linda Fraser
senior editor Margaret Malone
designer Mark Latter
photography by Steve Baxter, Michelle Garrett, William Lingwood and Craig Robertson
recipes by Joanna Farrow, Christine France, Brian Glover, Lucy Knox, Maggie Mayhew,
Jennie Shapter and Anne Sheasby
editorial reader Penelope Goodare
production controller Ben Worley

publisher's note

Although the advice and information in this book are believed to be accurate and true at the
time of going to press, neither the authors nor the publisher can accept any legal
responsibility or liability for any errors or omissions that may have been made nor for any
inaccuracies nor for any loss, harm or injury that comes about from following instructions or
advice in this book.

notes

Bracketed terms are intended for American readers. For all recipes, quantities are
given in both metric and imperial measures and, where appropriate, measures are also given
in standard cups and spoons. Follow one set, but not a mixture, because they are not
interchangeable. Standard spoon and cup measures are level. 1 tsp = 5ml, 1 tbsp = 15ml,
1 cup = 250ml/8fl oz. Australian standard tablespoons are 20ml. Australian readers should
use 3 tsp in place of 1 tbsp for measuring small quantities of sugar, spice, etc. Medium
(US large) eggs are used unless otherwise stated. The very young, the elderly, pregnant
women and those in ill-health or with a compromised immune system are advised against
consuming raw eggs or dishes and drinks containing raw eggs.

contents

introduction

There is something rather lovely about the warm and inviting aroma of pastry baking that conjures up memories of days gone by. I am sure many of us will admit that the simple jam tart was the first creation we brought triumphantly from the kitchen. This should reassure us that making tarts is not only simple but rewarding as well. Everyone reading this book should feel confident about their ability to achieve success. None of the recipes are difficult; a longer recipe does not suggest difficulty but merely that the process may take longer.

Once you have mastered the recipes in this book, why not mix and match pastries and fillings to create an infinite number of further creations of your own? A simple guide to making your own pastry can be found at the back of the book, but times have changed and sometimes, when time is short, even professional cooks reach for a packet of ready-made pastry. If you decide to opt for the ready-made fresh or frozen option, then simply use the pastry guide to check the quantity required.

Generally a tart is considered a dish with an undercrust only, whether this is pastry, bread or crumb, and it has no top. In the Middle Ages the undercrust would often serve as a plate. After the dinner had been eaten the plate was then devoured. The strict meaning therefore is "an open crust of the nature of a plate". The filling or topping can be as simple as a slice of prosciutto, some cherry tomatoes and a few pieces of goat's cheese baked on a round of puff pastry. Get out your rolling pin, put on your apron and get baking.

Maggie Mayhew

little tarts

Savoury tartlets make the perfect first course
for a meal, requiring little more than some crisp
salad leaves to make an instant impression.
Individual sweet tarts are ideal for dessert, or for
a treat with coffee at any time of day.

These full-flavoured little tartlets are baked with Mediterranean vegetables and chunks of tangy feta cheese. They are easy to make, so ideal for a quick morning snack.

tomato, feta and olive upside down tartlets

1 Preheat the oven to 200°C/400°F/Gas 6. Place the dried aubergine slices in a shallow dish. Pour over the boiling water and leave to soak for 10 minutes. Rinse in cold water, drain and dry on kitchen paper. Cut the aubergine slices in half or quarters, depending on their size.

2 Heat 30ml/2 tbsp of the sunflower or olive oil in a frying pan and fry the onion over a medium heat for 4–5 minutes. Add the mushrooms and cook for 3–4 minutes, or until the onions are just golden. Remove and set aside.

3 Heat the remaining oil in the frying pan, add the aubergine slices and garlic, and gently fry for 1–2 minutes. Lightly oil four individual shallow ovenproof dishes. Mix the halved tomatoes with the mushroom and onion mixture, aubergines, olives and feta cheese, and divide among the dishes. Season to taste with salt and pepper.

4 On a lightly floured surface, roll out the pastry thinly into an oblong, then cut out four rounds, each slightly larger than the diameter of the dishes. Place the pastry on top of the vegetable and cheese mixture, tucking any excess down inside the dish.

5 Bake for 20 minutes, or until the pastry is risen and golden. Cool slightly then invert on to individual warmed serving plates to serve.

simple serving

If you'd like to serve these tarts in their baking dishes, then turn each tartlet out on to a saucer before slipping it back into the hot dish.

serves 4

25g/1oz sun-dried aubergine (eggplant) slices

300ml/½ pint/1¼ cups boiling water

45ml/3 tbsp sunflower or olive oil

1 onion, thinly sliced

150g/5oz/2 cups button (white) mushrooms, thinly sliced

1 garlic clove, crushed

12–16 cherry tomatoes on the vine, halved

8 black or green olives, pitted and chopped

115g/4oz feta cheese, crumbled

flour, for dusting

350g/12oz ready-made puff pastry, thawed if frozen

salt and ground black pepper

These crisp and savoury mushroom tartlets are delicious served with some mixed gourmet salad leaves such as rocket, mizuna and red chard.

onion and mushroom tartlets

1 To make the pastry, sift the flour and cayenne into a bowl, add the butter, then rub in until the mixture looks like fine breadcrumbs. Stir in the Parmesan, then bind the pastry with enough of the water to make a firm dough. Wrap the pastry in clear film (plastic wrap) and chill for 45 minutes.

2 Heat 15ml/1 tbsp of the oil and half the butter in a heavy frying pan, then add the onions. Cover and cook gently for 15 minutes, stirring occasionally. Uncover the pan, increase the heat slightly and sprinkle in the sugar. Cook, stirring frequently, until the onions begin to caramelize and brown. Add the vinegar and soy sauce, and cook until the liquid evaporates. Set aside.

3 In a separate pan, heat 30ml/2 tbsp of the oil and the remaining butter. Add the mushrooms and garlic and cook for 5–6 minutes, or until browned. Stir the mushrooms into the onions with the tarragon and parsley. Season to taste. Preheat the oven to 190°C/375°F/Gas 5.

4 Roll out the pastry and use to line six 10cm/4in flan tins (mini-quiche pans). Prick the pastry with a fork and line with baking parchment and baking beans. Bake for 10 minutes, then remove the paper and beans and bake for 5–7 minutes more. Remove from the oven and increase the oven temperature to 200°C/400°F/Gas 6.

5 Remove the pastry shells from the tins, arrange them on a baking sheet and divide the vegetable mixture among them. Place one slice of goat's cheese on each tartlet. Drizzle with all the remaining oil and season with pepper. Return to the oven and bake for 5–8 minutes, or until the cheese is just golden. Serve with salad leaves.

serves 6

60ml/4 tbsp olive oil

25g/1oz/2 tbsp butter

4 red onions, thinly sliced

5ml/1 tsp soft light brown sugar

15ml/1 tbsp balsamic vinegar

15ml/1 tbsp soy sauce

200g/7oz/2½ cups button (white) mushrooms, thinly sliced

1 garlic clove, finely chopped

2.5ml/½ tsp chopped fresh tarragon

30ml/2 tbsp chopped fresh parsley

250g/9oz goat's cheese log (chèvre), cut into six slices

salt and ground black pepper

mixed salad leaves, to serve

for the pastry

200g/7oz/1¾ cups plain (all-purpose) flour, plus extra for dusting

pinch of cayenne pepper

90g/3½oz/7 tbsp butter, diced

40g/1½oz/½ cup grated Parmesan cheese

45–60ml/3–4 tbsp chilled water

Serve these brightly coloured individual tartlets as a first course. Alternatively, cook the filling ingredients in one large 23cm/9in tart case and serve slices as a main course.

leek, saffron, pepper and mussel tartlets

1 To make the pastry, sift the flour and salt into a large mixing bowl and add the butter. Rub the butter into the flour until the mixture resembles fine breadcrumbs. Lightly mix in just enough water to make the mixture hold together. Gather the dough together to form a ball, then wrap in clear film (plastic wrap) and chill for 30 minutes.

2 Preheat the oven to 190°C/375°F/Gas 5. Roll out the pastry and use to line six 10cm/4in flan tins (mini-quiche pans), 2.5cm/1in deep. Prick the bases and line with baking parchment and baking beans. Bake blind for 10 minutes. Remove the paper and beans and bake for 5–8 minutes, or until golden. Remove from the oven. Reduce the oven temperature to 180°C/350°F/Gas 4.

3 Soak the saffron in the hot water for 10 minutes. Soften the leeks in the oil in a large pan over a medium heat for 6–8 minutes, or until beginning to brown. Add the pepper strips and cook for another 2 minutes.

4 Bring 2.5cm/1in depth of water to a rolling boil in a pan and add 10ml/2 tsp salt. Discard any open mussels that do not shut when tapped sharply, then tip the rest into the pan. Cover and cook over a high heat, shaking the pan occasionally, for 3–4 minutes, or until the mussels open. Discard any mussels that do not open. Remove the mussel meat from the shells.

5 In a bowl, beat the eggs, cream and saffron liquid together. Season well with salt and pepper and whisk in the parsley. Arrange the leeks, peppers and mussels in the pastry cases. Pour the egg and cream mixture over and bake the tarts for 20–25 minutes, or until the filling is risen and just firm. Serve immediately with salad leaves.

serves 6

large pinch of saffron threads (about 15)

15ml/1 tbsp hot water

2 large leeks, sliced

30ml/2 tbsp olive oil

2 large yellow (bell) peppers, halved, seeded, grilled (broiled) and peeled, then cut into strips

900g/2lb fresh mussels, scrubbed and beards removed

2 large (US extra large) eggs

300ml/½ pint/1¼ cups single (light) cream

30ml/2 tbsp finely chopped fresh parsley

salt and ground black pepper

salad leaves, to serve

for the pastry

225g/8oz/2 cups plain (all-purpose) flour, plus extra for dusting

pinch of salt

115g/4oz/½ cup butter, diced

45–60ml/3–4 tbsp chilled water

These elegant and tangy tartlets are ideal for entertaining as the filling can be made the day before and chilled until needed.

smoked chicken with mayonnaise in filo

1 Preheat the oven to 200°C/400°F/Gas 6. Place the butter in a small pan and heat gently until melted. Lightly brush 12 mini flan rings with a little melted butter and set on a baking sheet.

2 Cut each sheet of filo pastry into 12 equal rounds large enough to line the rings and stand above the rims. Place a round of pastry in each ring and brush with a little melted butter, then add another round of pastry. Brush each with more butter and add a third round of pastry. Bake the tartlets for 5–10 minutes until golden. Leave in the rings for a few moments before transferring to a wire rack to cool.

3 Mix together the chicken, mayonnaise, lime rind and juice, peaches and seasoning. Chill for at least 30 minutes, but preferably overnight. When ready to serve, spoon the chicken mixture into the filo pastry cases and garnish with tarragon sprigs, lime slices and salad leaves.

makes 12

50g/2oz/¼ cup butter

3 sheets of filo pastry, each measuring about 45 × 28cm/18 × 11in, thawed if frozen

2 skinless, boneless smoked chicken breast fillets, finely sliced

150ml/¼ pint/⅔ cup mayonnaise

grated rind of 1 lime

30ml/2 tbsp lime juice

2 ripe peaches, peeled, stoned (pitted) and chopped

salt and ground black pepper

fresh tarragon sprigs, lime slices and salad leaves, to garnish

try tartlet tins

Mini flan rings make it easy to turn out the delicate filo shells but, if you don't have these, then you can use small tartlet tins (mini-quiche pans) instead.

These creamy little curd cheese tarts prove that certain traditions are well worth maintaining. Serve them with a cup of tea or coffee for a delightful afternoon break.

old-fashioned lemon curd cheesecake tarts

1 To make the pastry, sift the flour and salt into a large mixing bowl. Rub in the butter and lard or white vegetable fat until the mixture resembles fine breadcrumbs. Add the water to the dry ingredients and bring the mixture together using your fingertips to make a dough. Knead gently on a lightly floured work surface for a few seconds until smooth. Wrap the pastry in clear film (plastic wrap) and chill for 30 minutes.

2 Preheat the oven to 180°C/350°F/Gas 4. Roll out the pastry thinly, stamp out 24 rounds using a 7.5cm/3in plain pastry cutter and use to line two 12-cup tartlet tins (muffin pans) or cupcake tins (pans). Chill until required.

3 Use a wooden spoon to cream the curd cheese with the eggs, sugar and lemon rind in a bowl. Stir in the currants and brandy, if using. Place 2.5ml/ ½ tsp of the lemon curd in the base of each tartlet case. Spoon in the filling, smooth the tops slightly and bake for 40 minutes, or until just turning golden. Serve the tarts warm or cold, topped with whipped cream.

getting ahead

The pastry can be made in advance and frozen. Line the tins with pastry, wrap in clear film (plastic wrap) and freeze until required. Leave the pastry cases to thaw for about an hour before baking.

makes 24

225g/8oz/1 cup curd (farmer's) cheese

2 eggs, beaten

75g/3oz/6 tbsp caster (superfine) sugar

5ml/1 tsp finely grated lemon rind

50g/2oz/¼ cup currants

10ml/2 tsp brandy (optional)

60ml/4 tbsp lemon curd

whipped cream, to serve

for the pastry

275g/10oz/2½ cups plain (all-purpose) flour, plus extra for dusting

pinch of salt

75g/3oz/6 tbsp butter, diced

50g/2oz/¼ cup lard or white vegetable fat, diced

45–60ml/3–4 tbsp chilled water

The combination of rich, dark chocolate pastry and creamy white chocolate filling works perfectly in these elegant little tarts.

chocolate mousse tartlets

1 To make the pastry, sift the flour, sugar and cocoa powder into a mixing bowl. Rub in the butter using your fingertips until the mixture resembles fine breadcrumbs.

2 Mix together the eggs and vanilla essence in a small bowl, then add to the dry ingredients and mix to a soft dough. Tip out on to a lightly floured surface and bring together with your fingertips until smooth. Wrap in clear film (plastic wrap) and chill for 20 minutes.

3 Roll out the pastry and use to line six deep 10cm/4in loose-based flan tins (mini-quiche pans). Cover and chill for a further 20 minutes. Meanwhile, preheat the oven to 190°C/375°F/Gas 5.

4 Prick the base of each pastry case all over using a fork, then line with baking parchment and fill with baking beans. Bake blind for 10 minutes. Remove the paper and beans, return the cases to the oven and bake for a further 10–15 minutes, or until the pastry is cooked. Cool completely in the tins, and then turn out the pastry cases.

5 Melt the white chocolate in a small heatproof bowl set over a pan of hot water. Pour the milk into a separate pan, sprinkle over the gelatine and heat gently, stirring, until all the gelatine has dissolved. Remove the pan from the heat and stir in the melted white chocolate.

6 Whisk together the sugar, vanilla essence and egg yolks in a large mixing bowl, then beat in the white chocolate mixture. Beat in the yogurt until evenly mixed. Chill until beginning to set.

7 Whisk the egg whites in a grease-free bowl until stiff, then gently fold into the mixture. Divide among the pastry cases and leave to set. Drizzle the melted dark chocolate over the tartlets in a random pattern, to decorate.

makes 6

200g/7oz white chocolate, broken up

120ml/4fl oz/½ cup milk

10ml/2 tsp powdered gelatine

30ml/2 tbsp caster (superfine) sugar

5ml/1 tsp vanilla essence (extract)

2 eggs, separated

250g/9oz/generous 1 cup Greek (US strained plain) yogurt

melted dark (bitter sweet) chocolate, for drizzling

for the pastry

115g/4oz/1 cup plain (all-purpose) flour, plus extra for dusting

25g/1oz/2 tbsp icing (confectioners') sugar

25g/1oz/¼ cup cocoa powder (unsweetened)

75g/3oz/6 tbsp butter, diced

2 eggs, beaten

2.5ml/½ tsp vanilla essence (extract)

perfect pattern

A small paper piping bag is the best way to drizzle the melted chocolate over the tartlets, but you could simply pour the chocolate from the tip of a teaspoon.

Sharp tasting redcurrants and sweet peaches make a colourful topping for these simple filo pastry tartlets with a creamy yogurt filling.

peach and redcurrant tartlets

1 Preheat the oven to 190°C/375°F/Gas 5. Use a little of the butter to lightly grease four individual tartlet tins (mini-quiche pans). Brush the pastry squares with a little more butter, stack them in fours, then place them in the tartlet tins to make four pastry cases.

2 Bake on the centre shelf of the oven for about 15 minutes, or until golden. (Watch them carefully to make sure that they don't burn.) Cool the filo cases on a wire rack before removing them from the tins.

3 To make the filling, whip the cream to soft peaks, then lightly fold in the yogurt with the vanilla essence and the sifted icing sugar. Divide the mixture among the pastry cases.

4 Slice the peaches and arrange the slices on top of the filling, with a few redcurrants. Decorate each tartlet with a redcurrant sprig and lightly dust with icing sugar.

easy stripping
To remove redcurrants from their stalks, gently pull the stalks through the tines of a fork.

makes 4
25g/1oz/2 tbsp butter, melted

16 sheets of filo pastry, each measuring 15cm/6in square, thawed if frozen

150ml/¼ pint/⅔ cup double (heavy) cream

130g/4½oz/generous ½ cup peach and mango yogurt

few drops of vanilla essence (extract)

15ml/1 tbsp icing (confectioners') sugar, sifted, plus extra for dusting

2 peaches, halved and stoned (pitted)

50g/2oz/½ cup redcurrants, plus 4 redcurrant sprigs, to decorate

Simplicity is the key to these delightful pear-shaped tartlets. They are topped with a luscious chocolate sauce that complements the fruit beautifully.

poached pear tartlets with chocolate sauce

1 Cut the pears in half and scoop out the cores with a melon baller or small spoon, leaving the stalks. Put the water in a pan with the orange rind, vanilla pod, bay leaf and sugar, and bring to the boil. Add the pears and more water to cover, then reduce the heat and cook gently for 15 minutes. Remove the pears and set aside. Reserve the syrup.

2 Meanwhile, roll out the pastry on a lightly floured work surface and cut out six pear shapes, slightly larger than the pear halves. Place the pastry shapes on a greased baking sheet and chill for 30 minutes.

3 Remove the flavourings from the syrup, then return it to the heat. Boil rapidly for 10 minutes. Blend the cocoa powder with 60ml/4 tbsp cold water in a pan. Stir a little of the syrup into the cocoa paste, then whisk the paste into the syrup in the pan. Cook until reduced to about 150ml/ ¼ pint/⅔ cup. Remove the pan from the heat and stir in the cream.

4 Preheat the oven to 200°C/400°F/Gas 6. Pat the pears dry with kitchen paper. In a small bowl, mix together the butter, sugar and walnuts, then spoon a little into each pear cavity.

5 Lightly brush the pastry shapes with a little egg. Put a pear half, filled side down, in the centre of each pastry shape. Lightly sprinkle the pastries with a little caster sugar. Bake for 12 minutes, or until the pastry has puffed up around the pear and is golden brown. Drizzle over some of the warm chocolate sauce and serve immediately.

makes 6

3 firm pears, peeled
450ml/¾ pint/scant 2 cups water
strip of thinly pared orange rind
1 vanilla pod (bean)
1 bay leaf
50g/2oz/¼ cup granulated sugar
350g/12oz puff pastry, thawed if frozen
flour, for dusting
40g/1½oz/⅓ cup cocoa powder (unsweetened)

75ml/5 tbsp double (heavy) cream
15g/½oz/1 tbsp butter, softened
15ml/1 tbsp soft light brown sugar
25g/1oz/¼ cup walnuts, chopped
1 egg, beaten
15g/½oz/1 tbsp caster (superfine) sugar

lunchtime tarts

Whether you are looking for an easy but
impressive picnic dish or something delicious
to serve to friends at an impromptu lunch
party, there is a host of fabulous ideas to
choose from in this section.

Mild-flavoured leeks go exceptionally well with the salty taste of the Roquefort cheese, while the nuttiness of the walnut pastry complements them both.

roquefort and leek tart with walnut pastry

1 To make the pastry, sift the flour and 2.5ml/½ tsp salt into a mixing bowl. Add some black pepper and the sugar. Rub in the butter with your fingertips until the mixture resembles fine breadcrumbs, then add the ground walnuts and stir well. Add the lemon juice and chilled water and use your fingertips to bind and form a dough. Wrap in clear film (plastic wrap) and chill for about 30 minutes.

2 Preheat the oven to 190°C/375°F/Gas 5. Roll out the pastry thinly and use to line a 23cm/9in loose-based flan tin (quiche pan).

3 Protect the sides of the pastry case with a thin strip of foil. Prick the base all over with a fork and bake for 15 minutes. Remove the foil and bake the pastry case for 10 minutes more, or until golden and just firm to the touch. Reduce the oven temperature to 180°C/350°F/Gas 4.

4 To make the filling, melt the butter in a pan, add the leeks, then cover and cook on a low heat for 10 minutes, stirring occasionally. Season and cook for a further 10 minutes until soft. Set aside to cool.

5 Spoon the leeks into the pastry case, spreading them evenly, and arrange the slices of Roquefort cheese on top. Beat the eggs with the cream in a small bowl, and season with plenty of black pepper. Beat in the tarragon and carefully pour the mixture into the pastry case, covering the leek filling evenly.

6 Bake the tart on the centre shelf of the oven for 30–40 minutes, or until the filling has risen and browned and become firm to the touch. Allow to cool for 10 minutes before serving.

serves 4–6

25g/1oz/2 tbsp butter

450g/1lb leeks (trimmed weight), sliced

175g/6oz Roquefort cheese, thinly sliced

2 large (US extra large) eggs

250ml/8fl oz/1 cup double (heavy) cream

10ml/2 tsp chopped fresh tarragon

salt and ground black pepper

for the pastry

175g/6oz/1½ cups plain (all-purpose) flour, plus extra for dusting

5ml/1 tsp soft dark brown sugar

50g/2oz/¼ cup butter, diced

75g/3oz/¾ cup walnuts, ground

15ml/1 tbsp lemon juice

30ml/2 tbsp chilled water

cheese change

Other strong-tasting cheeses would be good in this tart – try Gruyère or a mature Cheddar.

Aubergines layered with spinach, feta cheese and rice combine to produce a satisfying and flavoursome tart, which will be popular with vegetarians and meat eaters alike.

greek feta tart

1 To make the pastry, sift the flour and salt into a large mixing bowl. Stir in the basil, then rub in the butter using your fingertips until the mixture resembles fine breadcrumbs. Sprinkle over most of the water and mix to form a dough, adding more water if required. Wrap in clear film (plastic wrap) and chill for about 30 minutes. Roll out the pastry thinly and use to line a deep 25cm/10in flan tin (quiche pan). Chill for 30 minutes.

2 Preheat the oven to 180°C/350°F/Gas 4. Prick the base of the chilled pastry case all over with a fork, then line with baking parchment and fill with baking beans. Bake blind for 10 minutes. Remove the paper and beans and return to the oven for 10 minutes.

3 To make the filling, heat 45ml/3 tbsp of the oil in a frying pan and fry the aubergine slices for 6–8 minutes on each side until golden. Drain the aubergine slices on kitchen paper. Add the onion and garlic to the oil remaining in the pan and fry over a gentle heat for 4–5 minutes until soft, adding a little extra oil if necessary. Wash the spinach, then chop it finely, by hand or in a food processor. Beat the eggs in a large mixing bowl.

4 Add the spinach, feta, Parmesan, yogurt, milk and the onion mixture to the eggs. Season to taste and stir thoroughly. Spread the cooked rice in an even layer over the base of the pastry case. Reserve about 8 aubergine slices, and arrange the rest in an even layer over the rice.

5 Spoon the spinach mixture over the aubergines and place the reserved slices of aubergine on top. Bake the tart for 30–40 minutes until lightly browned. Let the tart rest for 5 minutes before removing from the tin and serving.

serves 6

45–60ml/3–4 tbsp olive oil

1 large aubergine (eggplant), sliced

1 onion, chopped

1 garlic clove, crushed

175g/6oz fresh spinach

4 eggs

75g/3oz feta cheese, crumbled

40g/1½oz/½ cup freshly grated Parmesan cheese

60ml/4 tbsp natural (plain) yogurt

90ml/6 tbsp creamy milk

225g/8oz/2 cups cooked long grain rice

salt and ground black pepper

for the pastry

225g/8oz/2 cups plain (all-purpose) flour, plus extra for dusting

pinch of salt

5ml/1 tsp dried basil

115g/4oz/½ cup butter, diced

45–60ml/3–4 tbsp chilled water

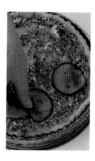

Potato pastry makes a great crust for a tart. Prepared with a creamy smoked salmon and caper filling, it makes a fantastic lunch.

smoked salmon tart with potato pastry

1 To make the pastry, cook the diced potato in a pan of lightly salted boiling water for 15 minutes. Drain well, then mash until smooth and set aside to cool.

2 Sift the flour into a large bowl and rub in the butter with your fingertips until the mixture resembles fine breadcrumbs. Beat in the potato and egg. Bring the mixture together, adding a little water if needed. Roll out the pastry on a lightly floured work surface and use to line a deep 23cm/9in round, loose-based, fluted flan tin (quiche pan). Chill for 1 hour.

3 Preheat the oven to 200°C/400°F/Gas 6 and place a heavy baking sheet in the oven to preheat. To make the filling, beat the eggs, milk and cream together in a bowl. Stir in the dill and capers and season. Stir in the salmon. Prick the pastry case with a fork and pour in the salmon mixture. Place on the baking sheet and bake for 35–45 minutes, or until the filling is just set and the crust is golden brown. Serve warm with mixed salad leaves and dill.

serves 6

6 eggs, beaten

150ml/¼ pint/⅔ cup creamy milk

300ml/½ pint/1¼ cups double (heavy) cream

30–45ml/2–3 tbsp chopped fresh dill

30ml/2 tbsp bottled capers, drained and chopped

275g/10oz smoked salmon slices, roughly chopped

salt and ground black pepper

salad leaves and chopped fresh dill, to serve

for the pastry

1 floury potato, about 115g/4oz, roughly diced

225g/8oz/2 cups plain (all-purpose) flour, plus extra for dusting

115g/4oz/½ cup butter, diced

½ egg, beaten

about 10ml/2 tsp chilled water

This classic onion and anchovy tart originates from Nice in southern France, and is sold in markets all over the region. This version is made with a delicious polenta dough.

pissaladière

1 To make the dough, mix the flour, polenta or semolina and salt in a large mixing bowl. Pour half the water into a bowl. Add the dried yeast and sugar, then leave in a warm place for 10 minutes, until frothy. Pour the yeast mixture into the flour with the remaining water and the olive oil.

2 Mix all the ingredients together to form a dough, then turn out and knead for 5 minutes, or until smooth, springy and elastic. Place the dough in an oiled plastic bag, then set aside at room temperature for 30–60 minutes until doubled in size.

3 To make the topping, heat 45ml/3 tbsp of the olive oil in a large, heavy pan and add the onions. Stir well to coat the onions in the oil, then cover and cook over a very low heat, stirring occasionally, for 20–30 minutes.

4 Add a little salt to taste, then the garlic, chopped thyme and 1 rosemary sprig. Stir well and cook for another 15–25 minutes, or until the onions are soft and deep golden yellow but not browned at all. Uncover the pan for the last 5–10 minutes if the onions seem very wet. Discard the rosemary, then set the onions aside to cool.

5 Preheat the oven to 220°C/425°F/Gas 7. Roll out the dough thinly and use to line a large baking sheet, about 30 × 23–25cm/12 × 9–10in. Spread the onions over the dough.

6 Arrange the anchovies in an even lattice pattern over the onions. Scatter the olives, thyme and rosemary leaves over the top of the pissaladière and drizzle with the remaining olive oil. Bake for about 25 minutes, or until the dough is browned and cooked. Season with pepper and serve warm.

serves 6

60–75ml/4–5 tbsp extra virgin olive oil

6 large sweet Spanish onions, thinly sliced

2 large garlic cloves, thinly sliced

5ml/1 tsp chopped fresh thyme, plus several sprigs

2 fresh rosemary sprigs

1–2 × 50g/2oz cans anchovies in olive oil, drained and halved lengthways

50–75g/2–3oz/⅓–½ cup small black olives, preferably small Niçoise olives

salt and ground black pepper

for the dough

250g/9oz/2¼ cups strong white bread flour, plus extra for dusting

50g/2oz/½ cup fine polenta or semolina

5ml/1 tsp salt

175ml/6fl oz/¾ cup lukewarm water

5ml/1 tsp dried yeast

5ml/1 tsp caster (superfine) sugar

30ml/2 tbsp extra virgin olive oil

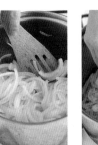

This pretty dessert is a great way to enjoy fresh apricots when they are in season. It's a delightful combination of fruit, almond filling and crumbly shortcrust pastry.

apricot and almond tart

1 To make the pastry, sift the flour and salt into a large mixing bowl and add the butter. Rub the butter into the flour using your fingertips until the mixture resembles fine breadcrumbs. Sprinkle over enough water to just hold the mixture together. Gather the dough together to form a ball, then wrap in clear film (plastic wrap) and chill for 30 minutes.

2 Preheat the oven to 180°C/350°F/Gas 4. Roll out the pastry thinly and use to line a 23cm/9in loose-based flan tin (quiche pan). Chill for 30 minutes.

3 To make the almond filling, place the butter and sugar in a mixing bowl and cream together, using a wooden spoon, until the mixture is light and fluffy.

4 Gradually add the beaten egg to the butter mixture, beating well after each addition. Gently fold in the ground rice, almonds and almond essence, and mix well to incorporate them.

5 Spoon the almond mixture into the pastry case, spreading it evenly, then arrange the apricot halves cut side down on top. Press them down gently.

6 Place the tart on a baking sheet and bake for about 45 minutes until the filling and pastry are cooked and lightly browned. Serve warm or cold, dusted with icing sugar and decorated with apricot slices and sprigs of mint, if you like.

for a change of flavour
Use ground hazelnuts and vanilla essence in place of the ground almonds and almond essence.

serves 6

115g/4oz/½ cup butter

115g/4oz/generous ½ cup caster (superfine) sugar

1 egg, beaten

50g/2oz/⅓ cup ground rice

50g/2oz/½ cup ground almonds

few drops of almond essence (extract)

450g/1lb fresh apricots, peeled, halved and stoned (pitted)

sifted icing (confectioners') sugar, for dusting (optional)

apricot slices and fresh mint sprigs, to decorate (optional)

for the pastry

225g/8oz/2 cups plain (all-purpose) flour, plus extra for dusting

pinch of salt

115g/4oz/½ cup butter, diced

45–60ml/3–4 tbsp chilled water

Use really ripe, sweet plums for this tart to ensure the best results. It is rich and smooth, and needs no more than a dollop of cream or ice cream to make it truly scrumptious.

egg custard tart with plums and almonds

1 To make the pastry, place the flour, salt, sugar, butter and egg in a food processor and process until thoroughly combined. Turn out the mixture on to a clean, lightly floured surface and bring it together. Wrap the pastry in clear film (plastic wrap) and chill for 30 minutes.

2 Flour a deep 18cm/7in square or 20cm/8in round loose-based cake tin (pan). Roll out the pastry and use to line the tin. This pastry is soft at this stage, so do not worry if you have to push it into the sides of the tin. Chill for a further 10–20 minutes.

3 Preheat the oven to 200°C/400°F/Gas 6. Line the pastry case with baking parchment and baking beans, then bake blind for 15 minutes. Remove the paper and beans, reduce the oven temperature to 180°C/350°F/Gas 4 and bake for a further 5–10 minutes until the base is dry.

4 Halve the plums and remove the stones (pits), and arrange the plums neatly, cut side down, in the pastry case. Whisk together the egg and egg yolks in a small bowl with the sugar, milk and vanilla essence, then carefully pour this custard mixture over the fruit.

5 Return the tart to the oven and bake for 25–30 minutes. When the custard is just firm to the touch, remove the tart from the oven and allow to cool. Sprinkle the flaked almonds evenly over the top and dredge with icing sugar before serving with cream or ice cream.

fruit and pastry variations

This tart is equally delicious made with fresh apricots, peaches or nectarines. Make a nutty pastry by replacing 15ml/1 tbsp of the flour with ground almonds or toasted ground hazelnuts.

serves 4–6

350g/12oz ripe plums

1 egg, plus 2 yolks

30ml/2 tbsp caster (superfine) sugar

300ml/½ pint/1¼ cups milk

few drops of vanilla essence (extract)

toasted flaked (sliced) almonds and sifted icing (confectioners') sugar, to decorate

thick cream or ice cream, to serve

for the pastry

175g/6oz/1½ cups plain (all-purpose) flour, plus extra for dusting

pinch of salt

15ml/1 tbsp caster (superfine) sugar

115g/4oz/½ cup unsalted (sweet) butter, diced

1 egg

This recipe recalls the flavours of the sunny Mediterranean with its mixture of pine nuts, lemon and honey. Use a good, flower-scented honey if you can.

honey and pine nut tart

1 Preheat the oven to 180°C/350°F/Gas 4. To make the pastry, sift the flour into a large mixing bowl and rub in the butter with your fingertips until the mixture resembles fine breadcrumbs.

2 Stir the icing sugar into the mixture. Add the egg and water and mix to form a soft dough. On a floured work surface, knead the dough lightly with your fingertips until smooth.

3 Roll out the pastry thinly and use to line a 23cm/9in flan tin (quiche pan). Prick the base with a fork, then chill for 10 minutes. Line the pastry case with baking parchment and fill with baking beans. Bake for 10 minutes. Remove the parchment and beans and set the pastry case aside while you prepare the filling.

4 In a large bowl, cream the butter and caster sugar together until light and fluffy. Add the eggs one at a time, beating well after each addition, then add the honey with the lemon rind and juice and mix well. Stir in the pine nuts and salt, blending well, then pour the filling evenly into the pastry case.

5 Bake for 45 minutes, or until the filling is lightly browned and set. Leave the tart to cool slightly in the tin, then remove and dust generously with icing sugar. Serve warm, or at room temperature, with crème fraîche, yogurt or vanilla ice cream, if you like.

serves 6

115g/4oz/½ cup butter, diced

115g/4oz/generous ½ cup caster (superfine) sugar

3 eggs, beaten

175g/6oz/¾ cup clear honey

grated rind and juice of 1 lemon

225g/8oz/2⅔ cups pine nuts

pinch of salt

a little sifted icing (confectioners') sugar, for dusting

crème fraîche, natural (plain) yogurt or vanilla ice cream, to serve

for the pastry

225g/8oz/2 cups plain (all-purpose) flour, plus extra for dusting

115g/4oz/½ cup butter, diced

30ml/2 tbsp icing (confectioners') sugar

1 egg, beaten

15ml/1 tbsp chilled water

This fabulous tart combines sweet Middle Eastern ingredients with a traditional shortcrust pastry to produce an unusual but delicious dessert.

date and almond tart with apricot glaze

1 Preheat the oven to 200°C/400°F/Gas 6 and place a baking sheet in the oven to preheat. To make the pastry, sift the flour into a bowl, then rub in the butter with your fingertips until the mixture resembles fine breadcrumbs. Add the egg and water, then use your fingertips to bring the mixture together into a dough. Wrap in clear film (plastic wrap) and chill for 30 minutes.

2 Roll out the pastry on a lightly floured work surface and use to line a 20cm/8in flan tin (quiche pan). Prick the base of the pastry case with a fork, then chill until required.

3 Cream the butter and sugar together in a mixing bowl with a wooden spoon until light, then beat in the egg. Stir in the ground almonds, flour and 15ml/1 tbsp of the orange flower water and mix well.

4 Spread the almond filling evenly over the base of the pastry case. Arrange the dates, cut side down, on the mixture.

5 Bake the tart on the hot baking sheet for about 15 minutes, then lower the oven temperature to 180°C/350°F/Gas 4. Bake the tart for 15 minutes more, or until pale golden and set.

6 Place the tart, in its tin, on a wire rack to cool. In a small pan, gently heat the apricot jam, then press through a sieve into a bowl. Stir in the remaining orange flower water. Generously brush the apricot glaze over the tart, carefully transfer it to a serving plate and serve at room temperature.

serves 6

90g/3½oz/7 tbsp butter, softened at room temperature

90g/3½oz/½ cup caster (superfine) sugar

1 egg, beaten

90g/3½oz/scant 1 cup ground almonds

30ml/2 tbsp plain (all-purpose) flour

30ml/2 tbsp orange flower water

12–13 fresh dates, halved and stoned (pitted)

60ml/4 tbsp apricot jam

for the pastry

175g/6oz/1½ cups plain (all-purpose) flour, plus extra for dusting

75g/3oz/6 tbsp butter, diced

1 egg

15ml/1 tbsp chilled water

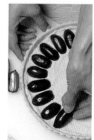

fancy tarts

When entertaining, or when you just feel like
being indulgent, these sophisticated tarts are
the ideal choice. Thankfully, none of the ideas
in this chapter mean spending hours in the
kitchen to create them.

This stunning tart really lets the ingredients speak for themselves: wild mushrooms and broccoli add flavour and colour to a robust potato and cheese pastry base.

wild mushroom and broccoli tart with cheese pastry

1 First make the pastry. Place the rice flour, cornmeal and salt in a mixing bowl and stir to mix. Lightly rub in the butter with your fingertips until the mixture resembles breadcrumbs.

2 Stir in the mashed potatoes and cheese and mix well to form a soft dough. Wrap the pastry in clear film (plastic wrap) and chill for 30 minutes.

3 Roll out the pastry between two sheets of baking parchment and use to line a 24cm/9½in loose-based flan tin (quiche pan), gently pressing the pastry into the sides of the flan tin. Carefully trim around the top edge of the pastry case with a sharp knife, and chill.

4 Preheat the oven to 200°C/400°F/Gas 6. Cook the broccoli florets in a large pan of lightly salted, boiling water for about 3 minutes, or until just tender. Drain the broccoli well and then set aside to cool.

5 Heat the oil in a frying pan, add the shallots and cook gently for 3 minutes. Add the mushrooms and cook for 2 minutes.

6 Spoon the shallots and mushrooms into the pastry case and top with the broccoli. Beat together the eggs, milk, tarragon and seasoning in a bowl and pour over the vegetables. Top with cheese. Bake for 10 minutes, then reduce the oven temperature to 180°C/350°F/Gas 4 and bake for 30 minutes, or until lightly set. Serve warm or cold, garnished with fresh herbs.

serves 8

115g/4oz small broccoli florets

15ml/1 tbsp olive oil

3 shallots, finely chopped

175g/6oz mixed wild mushrooms, such as ceps, shiitake and oyster mushrooms, sliced or chopped

2 eggs

200ml/7fl oz/scant 1 cup semi-skimmed (low-fat) milk

15ml/1 tbsp chopped fresh tarragon

50g/2oz/½ cup grated Cheddar cheese

salt and ground black pepper

fresh herbs, to garnish

for the pastry

75g/3oz/⅔ cup brown rice flour

75g/3oz/¾ cup fine cornmeal

pinch of salt

75g/3oz/6 tbsp butter, diced

115g/4oz cold mashed potatoes

50g/2oz/½ cup grated Cheddar cheese

This savoury version of the famous French apple tarte tatin has caramelized shallots baked under a layer of crisp Parmesan pastry, producing a rich and surprisingly filling tart.

shallot and garlic tarte tatin with parmesan pastry

1 To make the pastry, roll out the ready-made puff pastry thinly into a long rectangle, on a floured work surface. Spread the butter over it, leaving a 2.5cm/1in border. Scatter the Parmesan cheese on top. Fold the bottom third of the pastry up to cover the middle and the top third down. Seal the edges, give the pastry a quarter turn and then roll out to a long rectangle. Fold the pastry once more and chill for 30 minutes.

2 To make the filling, melt the butter in a 23–25cm/9–10in round heavy frying pan or skillet that will go in the oven. Add the shallots and garlic cloves, and cook until lightly browned all over.

3 Scatter the sugar over the top and increase the heat a little. Cook until the sugar begins to caramelize, then turn the shallots and garlic in the buttery juices, coating them thoroughly. Add the balsamic or sherry vinegar, water, thyme and seasoning. Cook the shallots and garlic, part-covered, for about 5 minutes, or until the garlic cloves are tender. Remove the pan from the heat and leave to cool.

4 Preheat the oven to 190°C/375°F/Gas 5. Roll out the pastry slightly larger than the diameter of the pan or skillet and lay it over the shallots and garlic, tucking the edges in. Prick the pastry with the point of a sharp knife, then bake for 25–35 minutes, or until the pastry is risen and golden.

5 Leave to cool for 5–10 minutes, then invert the tart on to a serving plate. Scatter with a few thyme sprigs, if you like, and serve.

serves 4–6

40g/1½oz/3 tbsp butter
500g/1¼lb shallots
12–16 large garlic cloves, peeled but left whole
15ml/1 tbsp golden caster (superfine) sugar
15ml/1 tbsp balsamic or sherry vinegar
45ml/3 tbsp water
5ml/1 tsp chopped fresh thyme, plus a few extra sprigs, to garnish (optional)
salt and ground black pepper

for the pastry

300g/11oz puff pastry, thawed if frozen
flour, for dusting
50g/2oz/¼ cup butter, softened
75g/3oz/1 cup freshly grated Parmesan cheese

Wonderfully mild and sweet when cooked, red onions go especially well with creamy fontina cheese and spicy sausage in this tart made with a cornmeal crust.

red onion and sausage tart

1 To make the pastry, sift the plain flour and cornmeal into a bowl with 5ml/1 tsp salt. Add plenty of pepper and stir in the sugar and thyme. Rub in the butter with your fingertips until the mixture looks like breadcrumbs. Beat the egg yolk with 30ml/2 tbsp iced water and use to bind the pastry, adding another 15ml/1 tbsp iced water, if necessary. Gather the dough into a ball, wrap in clear film (plastic wrap) and chill for 30 minutes.

2 To make the filling, heat 45ml/3 tbsp of the oil in a large, deep frying pan and add the onions. Cover and cook slowly, stirring occasionally, for 20–30 minutes. The onions should soften but not brown.

3 Add the garlic and chopped thyme, and crumble in the spicy sausage. Cook, stirring occasionally, for another 10 minutes. Increase the heat slightly, then add the sugar and sherry vinegar. Cook, uncovered, for 5 minutes more, or until the onions start to caramelize slightly. Season and allow to cool.

4 Preheat the oven to 190°C/375°F/Gas 5. Roll out the pastry thinly and use to line a 25cm/10in loose-based flan tin (quiche pan).

5 Prick the pastry all over with a fork, then line with baking parchment and fill with baking beans. Bake for 10 minutes. Remove the paper and beans and return the pastry case to the oven for 5 minutes until lightly coloured.

6 Spread the onions and sausage over the base of the pastry case. Add the fontina slices and some sprigs of thyme, and season with pepper. Drizzle over the remaining oil, then bake for 15–20 minutes, or until the filling is hot and the cheese is beginning to bubble. Garnish with thyme.

serves 4–6

60ml/4 tbsp olive oil

900g/2lb red onions, thinly sliced

2–3 garlic cloves, thinly sliced

5ml/1 tsp chopped fresh thyme, plus a few whole sprigs to garnish

115g/4oz spicy sausage, skinned

5ml/1 tsp soft dark brown sugar

10ml/2 tsp sherry vinegar

225g/8oz fontina cheese, thinly sliced

salt and ground black pepper

for the pastry

115g/4oz/1 cup plain (all-purpose) flour, plus extra for dusting

75g/3oz/¾ cup fine yellow cornmeal

5ml/1 tsp dark brown sugar

5ml/1 tsp chopped fresh thyme

90g/3½oz/7 tbsp butter, diced

1 egg yolk

30–45ml/2–3 tbsp iced water

A simple crisp pastry case is all that is needed to set off this classic
filling of vanilla-flavoured custard topped with luscious berry fruits.

summer berry tart

1 To make the pastry, sift the flour and salt into a mixing bowl. Rub in the
butter until the mixture resembles fine breadcrumbs. Mix the egg yolk with
the chilled water and sprinkle over the dry ingredients. Gather the mixture
together until it forms a firm dough.

2 Put the dough on to a lightly floured surface and knead for a few seconds,
until smooth. Wrap in clear film (plastic wrap) and chill for 30 minutes.

3 Roll out the pastry and use to line a 25cm/10in fluted flan tin (quiche
pan). Wrap in clear film and chill for 30 minutes.

4 Put a baking sheet in the oven and preheat to 200°C/400°F/Gas 6. Prick the
base of the pastry, line with foil and baking beans and bake blind for 15 minutes.
Remove the foil and beans and bake for 10 minutes more. Leave to cool.

5 To make the custard, place the egg yolks, sugar, cornflour, flour and vanilla
essence in a bowl and beat well. Bring the milk to the boil in a pan, and
then slowly pour on to the egg mixture, whisking all the time. Pour the
custard into the cleaned pan and cook over a low
heat, stirring constantly, until it has thickened.
Return the custard to a clean mixing bowl, cover
the surface with clear film and set aside to cool.

6 Whip the cream until thick, then fold into the
custard. Spoon the custard into the pastry case
and spread out evenly, then arrange the fruit on
top of the custard. Gently heat the redcurrant
jelly and liqueur together in a small pan until
melted. Allow to cool, then brush evenly over the
fruit. Serve the tart within 3 hours of assembling,
decorated with mint, if using.

serves 6–8

3 egg yolks

50g/2oz/¼ cup caster
(superfine) sugar

30ml/2 tbsp cornflour
(cornstarch)

30ml/2 tbsp plain
(all-purpose) flour

5ml/1 tsp vanilla
essence (extract)

300ml/½ pint/1¼
cups milk

150ml/¼ pint/⅔ cup
double (heavy) cream

800g/1¾ lb/7 cups
summer berries, such
as boysenberries, rasp-
berries or blueberries

60ml/4 tbsp redcurrant
jelly

30ml/2 tbsp raspberry
liqueur

fresh mint leaves,
to decorate (optional)

for the pastry

185g/6½ oz/1½ cups
plain (all-purpose)
flour, plus extra for
dusting

pinch of salt

115g/4oz/½ cup
butter, diced

1 egg yolk

30ml/2 tbsp chilled
water

Beautifully scented fresh raspberries and a delectable crunchy caramel topping contrast with the thick vanilla custard filling in this lovely summery tart.

raspberry brûlée tart

1 To make the pastry, sift the flour, salt and icing sugar into a bowl. Rub in the butter using your fingertips until the mixture resembles fine breadcrumbs. Mix together the egg yolks and orange rind, add to the dry ingredients and mix to a soft dough. Knead the pastry with your fingertips on a lightly floured work surface for a few seconds until smooth. Wrap in clear film (plastic wrap) and chill for 30 minutes.

2 Roll out the pastry and use to line a fluted 23cm/9in flan tin (quiche pan). Wrap in clear film and chill for 30 minutes. Put a baking sheet in the oven and preheat to 200°C/400°F/Gas 6.

3 Prick the base of the pastry with a fork and line with foil and baking beans. Place on the hot baking sheet and bake for 10 minutes. Remove the foil and beans and bake the pastry for 5 minutes more. Lightly brush the base and sides of the pastry case with egg white, then return to the oven for 3–4 minutes. Lower the oven temperature to 160°C/325°F/Gas 3.

4 To make the custard, halve the vanilla pod lengthways. Place in a small pan with the cream. Slowly bring to the boil, then remove the vanilla pod. In a large bowl, whisk the egg and egg yolks with the sugar until pale. Slowly whisk in the hot cream.

5 Arrange the raspberries in the pastry case. Pour over the custard, then bake for 20 minutes, or until very lightly set. Place on a wire rack to cool, still in the tin. Chill for at least 4 hours, or overnight if possible.

6 To add the brûlée topping, first protect the edges of the pastry with pieces of foil. Dredge a thin layer of icing sugar over the custard. Grill (broil) for 1 minute, or until the sugar melts and turns golden. Take care not to over-grill or the custard will separate. Chill for 10 minutes before serving.

serves 8

1 vanilla pod (bean)

450ml/¾ pint/scant 2 cups double (heavy) cream

1 whole egg, plus 3 egg yolks

30ml/2 tbsp caster (superfine) sugar

150g/5oz/scant 1 cup fresh raspberries

75ml/5 tbsp icing (confectioners') sugar

for the pastry

150g/5oz/1¼ cups plain (all-purpose) flour, plus extra for dusting

pinch of salt

25g/1oz/¼ cup icing (confectioners') sugar

75g/3oz/6 tbsp butter, diced

2 egg yolks

finely grated rind of 1 orange

15ml/1 tbsp egg white, lightly beaten

perfect pastry

When rolling out the pastry, hold the edge of the pastry around the rolling pin over the far edge of the flan tin and carefully unroll the pastry towards you, allowing it to settle in the tin.

Coffee adds a new dimension to the frangipane filling in this elegant blueberry tart with its tangy citrus pastry case. The jam and liqueur glaze adds an indulgent finish.

blueberry frangipane flan

1 Preheat the oven to 190°C/375°F/Gas 5. To make the pastry, sift the flour into a large mixing bowl and rub in the butter using your fingertips until the mixture resembles fine breadcrumbs. Add the caster sugar and lemon rind, stir well, then add just enough water to form a soft but not sticky dough. Bring the dough together with your hands, then wrap in clear film (plastic wrap) and chill for about 20 minutes.

2 Roll out the pastry on a lightly floured surface and use to line a 23cm/9in loose-based flan tin (quiche pan). Prick the base with a fork. Line the pastry with baking parchment and fill with baking beans. Wrap in clear film and chill for 30 minutes. Bake for 10 minutes. Remove the baking parchment and beans and bake for 10 minutes more. Leave to cool.

3 While the pastry case is baking, mix the ground coffee and milk in a large mixing bowl. Leave to infuse for 4 minutes. Cream the butter and sugar until pale. Beat in the egg, then add the almonds and flour. Strain the milky coffee into the mixture through a fine sieve, and gently fold it in.

4 Spoon the coffee mixture into the pastry case and spread evenly. Scatter the blueberries over the top and push them down slightly into the mixture.

5 Bake for about 30 minutes until firm, covering the flan with foil after 20 minutes to prevent it getting too brown.

6 Remove the flan from the oven and allow to cool slightly. Melt the jam and liqueur in a small pan and brush over the flan. Remove the flan from the tin and serve warm with crème fraîche or sour cream.

careful cooking
It is important to let the milk infuse and cool slightly or it
may curdle the egg when it is added to the mixture in step 4.

serves 6
30ml/2 tbsp ground coffee

45ml/3 tbsp
near-boiling milk

50g/2oz/¼ cup butter,
softened

50g/2oz/¼ cup caster
(superfine) sugar

1 egg

115g/4oz/1 cup ground
almonds

15ml/1 tbsp plain
(all-purpose) flour

225g/8oz/2 cups
blueberries

30ml/2 tbsp seedless
blackberry jam

15ml/1 tbsp Amaretto
liqueur

crème fraîche or sour
cream, to serve

for the pastry
175g/6oz/1½ cups plain
(all-purpose flour), plus
extra for dusting

115g/4oz/½ cup butter,
diced

25g/1oz/2 tbsp caster
(superfine) sugar

finely grated rind of
½ lemon

about 15ml/1 tbsp
chilled water

Subtle ricotta becomes altogether something different when combined with chocolate chips and mixed peel baked in a chocolate and sherry pastry case.

chocolate ricotta tart

1 To make the pastry, sift the flour and cocoa powder into a mixing bowl, then stir in the sugar. Rub in the butter using your fingertips until the mixture resembles fine breadcrumbs, then work in the dry sherry, using your fingertips, to bind the mixture to a dough. Put the dough on a lightly floured work surface and knead for a few seconds until smooth.

2 Roll out three-quarters of the pastry on a lightly floured surface and use to line a 23cm/9in loose-based flan tin (quiche pan). Chill for 20 minutes. Preheat the oven to 200°C/400°F/Gas 6.

3 To make the filling, beat the egg yolks and sugar in a clean bowl, then add the ricotta cheese. Beat with a wooden spoon to mix thoroughly. Stir in the lemon rind, chocolate chips, mixed peel and angelica. Spoon the ricotta mixture into the pastry case and level the surface.

4 Roll out the remaining pastry and cut it into narrow strips, then arrange these in a lattice pattern over the filling. Bake for 15 minutes, then lower the oven temperature to 180°C/350°F/Gas 4.

5 Bake for 35 minutes more until the pastry is golden. Cool in the tin before serving.

processor pastry
You can make this pastry in a food processor. Place all the dry ingredients in the bowl of the machine, add the butter and pulse until the mixture resembles breadcrumbs. Sprinkle the sherry evenly over the surface and pulse again until the mixture just begins to form a dough.

serves 6

2 egg yolks

115g/4oz/generous ½ cup caster (superfine) sugar

500g/1¼lb/2½ cups ricotta cheese

finely grated rind of 1 lemon

90ml/6 tbsp dark (bittersweet) chocolate chips

75ml/5 tbsp chopped mixed peel

45ml/3 tbsp chopped angelica

for the pastry

225g/8oz/2 cups plain (all-purpose) flour, plus extra for dusting

30ml/2 tbsp cocoa powder (unsweetened)

60ml/4 tbsp caster (superfine) sugar

115g/4oz/½ cup butter, diced

60ml/4 tbsp dry sherry

cook's tip
This tart is best served at room temperature, so if you make it in advance, cool, then chill. Bring to room temperature before serving.

pastry techniques

Learning a few basic techniques involved in the creation of a tart should stop you feeling apprehensive about the art. Once perfected, your shortcrust and sweet pastry will be much better than the shop bought versions. Making filo and puff pastries however will challenge even the most accomplished of cooks, so here you shouldn't feel guilty about opening a packet when a recipe calls for it.

shortcrust pastry

This is the easiest and most versatile of the pastries and can be used for both sweet and savoury tarts. It's not a myth that people with cold hands make the best pastry so, if you have hot hands, then it really would be better to use a food processor either to simply do the rubbing in for you or to mix the pastry too. When making shortcrust, the only other things to remember are to ensure that the fat is used straight from the refrigerator, and to knead the pastry only very lightly using your fingertips rather than the palm of your hand.

makes 350g/12oz

225g/8oz/2 cups plain (all-purpose) flour

pinch of salt

115g/4oz/½ cup chilled butter, diced, or half butter and half white vegetable fat or lard, cut into small cubes

60ml/4 tbsp chilled water

1 Sift the flour and salt into a large mixing bowl. Add the butter and white vegetable fat or lard, if using, and use your fingertips to rub the fat into the flour until the mixture resembles fine breadcrumbs. (This process can be done in a food processor if you prefer.)

2 Sprinkle the water over the top of the mixture and use a round-bladed knife to stir the water into the mixture until it forms larger clumps. If the mixture is too dry, add a few drops more water and then mix again.

3 Use the fingertips of one hand to gather the mixture together so that it forms a ball. Knead the dough using your fingertips on a lightly floured work surface until the dough is smooth.

4 Wrap the dough in clear film (plastic wrap) and chill for about 30 minutes before using.

using a processor

1 Sift the flour and salt on to a sheet of paper, then tip it into the bowl of the processor.

2 Add the diced fat and, using the pulse button of the machine, process until the mixture resembles fine breadcrumbs.

3 Sprinkle the water evenly over the surface of the mixture and then pulse again until it just starts to bind together. Tip the mixture out on to a floured work surface and knead lightly before wrapping and chilling.

shortcrust variations

Now you've mastered making plain pastry, the basic method can be used to make flavoured dough to complement whatever filling you are using.

cheese pastry

Add 50g/2oz/½ cup grated mature Cheddar cheese or 45ml/3 tbsp freshly grated Parmesan cheese and a good pinch of dry English mustard powder to the rubbed-in mixture.

herby pastry

Add 15ml/1 tbsp dried mixed herbs or Herbes de Provence to the rubbed-in mixture. Use about 45ml/3 tbsp mixed chopped fresh herbs, such as chives, thyme and parsley, if you prefer.

rich shortcrust pastry

makes 400g/14oz

225g/8oz/2 cups plain
(all-purpose) flour

pinch of salt

150g/5oz/10 tbsp
chilled butter, diced

1 egg yolk

30ml/2 tbsp chilled water

This richer version of shortcrust pastry
has a higher proportion of fat and also
contains sugar and egg yolk.

1 Sift the flour and salt into a large
bowl. Rub in the butter until the
mixture resembles fine breadcrumbs.

2 Mix the egg yolk and water
together and add to the flour mixture.
Use a rounded knife to bring the
mixture together until it forms a
soft dough.

3 Knead gently on a lightly floured
surface until smooth. Wrap in clear film
(plastic wrap) and chill for 30 minutes.

light nut crust

For fruit tarts, add 40g/1½oz/⅓ cup
ground almonds, ground walnuts or
toasted ground hazelnuts to the flour
after rubbing in the butter.

pâte sucrée

This rich, crisp-textured sweet pastry is
sometimes known as biscuit pastry. It
is made in a slightly different way to
shortcrust, on a work surface, rather than
in a bowl, but you'll find that it really
isn't difficult to prepare and the result is
well worth the extra effort. Pâte sucrée
is slightly softer than shortcrust, so it is
trickier to handle when you are rolling
it out and lining tins, but, if it breaks,
any tears or holes can be easily patched
by pressing the dough together with
your fingertips.

makes about 275g/10oz

150g/5oz/1¼ cups plain
(all-purpose) flour

pinch of salt

75g/3oz/6 tbsp chilled,
unsalted (sweet) butter, diced

25g/1oz/¼ cup icing
(confectioners') sugar

2 egg yolks

1 Sift the flour and salt into a heap on
to a cold work surface. Make a well in
the centre of the flour and place the rest
of the ingredients into the well.

2 Using your fingertips only, gradually
draw the flour into the middle and work
it into the butter, sugar and yolks.

3 When all the flour has been
incorporated, press the dough into a
ball, then knead lightly.

4 Flatten the dough slightly using the
palm of your hand, then wrap it in clear
film (plastic wrap) and chill for at least
30 minutes before using.

top tips for pastry making

• Lift up the flour and butter as
you rub them in to incorporate
air into the mixture, which will
make your pastry lighter.

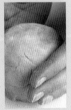

• Ensure the butter or fat you
use is chilled, but not too hard.
• Always use the tips of your
fingers when kneading pastry.
Excessive handling will develop
the gluten in the flour, which
will make the pastry tough.
• Allow plenty of time for the
pastry to chill and relax. This
will prevent it from shrinking
when it is baked.

quantity guide for tarts

The following guide shows the quantity of made pastry to use for each size of tin.

TIN SIZE	PASTRY WEIGHT
18cm/7in round	200g/7oz
20cm/8in round	275g/10oz
23cm/9in round	350g/12oz
25cm/10in round	400g/14oz
four, 10cm/4in tartlets	250g/9oz
six, 7.5cm/3in tartlets	250g/9oz

using pastry for tarts

Once your pastry has been made or bought you are ready to roll it out and line the tin or tins – just follow these few brief steps.

rolling out pastry

Whether the pastry is shortcrust or puff the same method of rolling should be used. Remember to keep everything as cool as possible. Try not to add too much flour when rolling, and always dust the work surface and the rolling pin rather than the pastry. Rotate the dough often to ensure that it rolls out evenly and doesn't stick to the work surface. Roll the pastry in one direction only, don't change the angle of your rolling pin, and try to avoid moving your body.

lining a tart tin

If you can, use a tart tin (quiche pan) that has a removable base so that the finished tart can be easily removed from the tin. Traditional tart tins will have straight sides – either fluted or plain – but many modern tins have slightly sloping sides.

1 Roll out the pastry on a lightly floured work surface to a thickness of about 3mm/$\frac{1}{8}$in (6mm/$\frac{1}{4}$in for pâte sucrée) and about 7.5cm/3in wider than the base of the tin, to allow for the depth of the tin.

2 To transfer the pastry to the tin, roll it around the rolling pin, then lift it and unroll it gently over the tin, taking care not to stretch it. Let the edges of the rolled-out dough rest over the sides of the tin.

3 Gently lift the edges of the dough and, without stretching the pastry, press it into the bottom edges of the tin with the other hand.

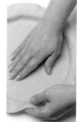

4 Allow any excess pastry to overlap the top of the tin. Roll the rolling pin over the top to cut off the excess and give a neat edge. Use the side of your finger to press the pastry into each of the curves if the tin is fluted and to increase the height of the rim slightly. This will allow for any shrinkage during cooking.

lining tartlet tins

When using tartlet tins, roll out all the pastry in one piece and use it to line all the tins in one go.

1 Place the tartlet tins (mini quiche pans) close together on a work surface. Roll out the pastry thinly until it is large enough to cover all the tins and drape it over the top.

2 Use a floured finger to ease the pastry into each of the tins, carefully pressing the pastry into the flutes. When all the tins are lined, roll a rolling pin over the top of them all to remove the excess pastry in one go.

baking pastry

Shortcrust-type pastry needs to be cooked at a high temperature of 200°C/400°F/Gas 6 for at least 15 minutes to allow it to crisp. Pastry containing sugar needs to be watched as it can burn quite quickly.

baking a tart shell blind

This process is often used when making tarts to either part-cook or cook the pastry fully to ensure it stays crisp once the filling has been added.

1 Prick the base of the pastry-lined tart tin (quiche pan) with a fork. Cut a round of baking parchment 7.5cm/3in larger than the tin and lay it over the pastry base and up the sides.

2 Fill with ceramic pastry beans or dried peas or beans and spread out evenly to cover the base.

3 Preheat the oven to 200°C/400°F/Gas 6, then bake the pastry case for 10 minutes.

4 Remove the paper and beans (allow the beans to cool and they can then be reused), then return the tart case to the oven for a further 5–10 minutes. This depends on whether it is to be baked further with a filling or not.

fillings for tarts

Fill a cooked pastry tart case with some crème patissière and fruit for a simple cold dessert. Alternatively use frangipane filling and top it with either fruit or nuts before baking.

crème patissière

This thickened sweet custard or pastry cream is the classic filling for fruit tarts and small pastries. It can be flavoured with chocolate, coffee or alcohol before using. This quantity will be enough to fill a 20cm/8in tart case.

1 Whisk 3 egg yolks with 50g/2oz/¼ cup caster (superfine) sugar and 40g/1½oz/6 tbsp plain (all-purpose) flour together in a bowl. Heat 250ml/8fl oz/1 cup of milk with a split vanilla pod (bean) over a low heat until almost boiling. Remove the vanilla pod and pour the milk into the egg yolks, whisking all the time.

2 Pour the mixture into a clean pan and bring to the boil, stirring all the time until thickened. Simmer for 2 minutes, then remove from the heat, cover the surface with a piece of clear film (plastic wrap) and cool.

3 When the custard is cold, spread it into a cooked pastry case before topping with the fruit of your choice.

frangipane filling

This almond sponge mixture can be topped with fruit or spooned on to a layer of jam in a part-baked pastry case prior to baking. This quantity will be enough to fill a 20cm/8in tart case.

1 Cream 25g/1oz/2 tbsp butter with 30ml/2 tbsp caster (superfine) sugar until pale, using a wooden spoon or electric hand whisk. Beat in 30ml/2 tbsp beaten egg, then lightly fold in 25g/1oz/¼ cup ground almonds and 15ml/1 tbsp plain (all-purpose) flour.

2 Spoon the mixture into a pastry case and spread evenly. Top with sliced fruit, berries or flaked (sliced) almonds, then bake in a preheated oven at 190°C/375°F/Gas 5 for 35–40 minutes. Leave to cool slightly, then brush the top with apricot jam glaze before serving.

index

Vesper

This recipe is the prototype James Bond mixture, popularized in *Casino Royale*. Bond named it after his girlfriend, "because once you've tasted it, that's all you want to drink".

3 measures/4¹/₂ tbsp gin
1 measure/1¹/₂ tbsp vodka
¹/₂ measure/2 tsp Lillet Blanc wine

Pour the ingredients into a cocktail shaker half-filled with cracked ice. Shake well, then strain into a chilled cocktail glass. Garnish with a twist of lemon.

Vodkatini

Bond later refined the Vesper recipe into this variation on the classic Dry Martini, with vodka replacing the gin. Famously, it should be "shaken, not stirred".

1 measure/1¹/₂ tbsp vodka
dash dry white vermouth

Shaking a Vodkatini gives the drink a cloudiness not achieved in the standard Dry Martini recipe. Since vodka lacks the aromatic character of gin, it is served with a twist of lemon rind immersed in the drink, as well as being squeezed over it.

Chilli Vodkatini

Not quite a Vodkatini, but almost. This recipe produces a hot, savoury drink that is stirred in the manner of the original Dry Martini, and served with a couple of chilli peppers in it.

1 measure/1¹/₂ tbsp chilli or pepper vodka
¹/₄ measure/1 tsp dry French vermouth
2 small pickled or vodka-soaked chillies and 1 pitted green olive, to garnish

1 Add the chilli or pepper vodka to a bar glass of ice and mix for about 30 seconds, until the outside of the glass is frosted over. Add the vermouth to a chilled cocktail glass, swirl it around to wet the inside of the glass, and then pour it away.

2 Cut one of the chillies in half and discard the seeds. Thread it through the olive, then thread the olive on to a cocktail stick with the other chilli. Strain the cocktail into the prepared glass. Add the decoration to the drink before serving.

Barbara

This is a variation on the White Russian, but with a chocolatey flavour replacing the original coffee.

1 measure/1½ tbsp vodka
1 measure/1½ tbsp white crème de cacao
½ measure/2 tsp double (heavy) cream

Shake all the ingredients well with ice, and strain into a cocktail glass. The surface of the drink can be sprinkled with grated chocolate.

Katinka

This fruity mixture achieves a nice balance of sweet and sour flavours, and is revved up with the added horsepower of the vodka. A good Russian brand such as Stolichnaya would be the optimum choice for the drink.

1¹/₂ measures/6 tsp vodka
1 measure/1¹/₂ tbsp apricot brandy
¹/₂ measure/2 tsp lime juice

Shake all the ingredients well with ice, and strain into a cocktail glass heaped with slivered ice. Add a slice of lime.

Ménage-à-Trois

Many modern cocktails have ice cream added to them. It gives a richer flavour and creamier texture, and makes for an altogether luxurious mixture. This is a particularly naughty example.

1 measure/1¹/₂ tbsp vodka
4 strawberries
1 measure/1¹/₂ tbsp coconut cream
30ml/2 tbsp rich chocolate
  ice cream

Add all the ingredients to a liquidizer with cracked ice and blend for 20 seconds or so, until the strawberries are quite pulverized. Strain into a chilled rocks glass. Garnish with another whole strawberry.

Cosmopolitan

This drink has a similar bracing flavour to a Sea Breeze, but the sweet liqueur shows through the bitter juices.

1¹/₂ measures/6 tsp vodka
1 measure/1¹/₂ tbsp Cointreau
1 measure/1¹/₂ tbsp cranberry juice
¹/₂ measure/2 tsp lime juice

Shake all the ingredients well with ice, and strain into a large cocktail glass. Dangle a twist of orange in the drink.

Après-Ski

Certainly not to be tried *before* skiing anyway. The intriguing mixture of aniseed, mint and lemon in this drink is quite a challenge. Somehow the mint emphasizes the flavour of the Pernod. One should be enough, not least because the drink has an exceedingly long aftertaste.

1 measure/1¹/₂ tbsp vodka
1 measure/1¹/₂ tbsp Pernod
¹/₂ measure/2 tsp green crème de menthe
5 measures/120ml/4fl oz sparkling lemonade

Shake the first three ingredients with ice, and then strain into a highball glass with a couple of ice cubes in it. Add the lemonade. Garnish the drink with a sprig of mint and a slice of lemon.

Bartending know-how
The principal flavouring element in crème de menthe – green or white – is peppermint. Its flavour is more subtly aromatic and refreshing than that of spearmint.

Harvey Wallbanger

This is the next step up from a Screwdriver, with a dash of Galliano added. It is a 1970s recipe that supposedly derives its name from having left a gentleman called Harvey, who had downed several of them, in the walking-into-walls state. There is no need to go quite that far, but it's easy to see why the formula became such a popular one in nightclubs.

2 measures/3 tbsp vodka
³/₄ measure/3 tsp Galliano
5 measures/120ml/4fl oz orange
   juice
1 orange

1 Pour the vodka, Galliano and orange juice into a pitcher half-filled with cracked ice. Mix the cocktail and ice for 30 seconds, to chill it well.

2 Using a canelle knife, take a series of strips of rind off the orange, running from the top to the bottom of the fruit.

3 Use a small sharp knife to cut the orange evenly and thinly into slices.

4 Cut the orange slices in half and wedge them between cracked ice in a highball glass.

5 Strain the chilled cocktail into the prepared glass.

Czarina

A recipe from the age when vodka was still enough
of a commercial novelty for a drink containing it to be
given a name with glamorous Russian connotations.

1 measure/1½ tbsp vodka
½ measure/2 tsp apricot brandy
½ measure/2 tsp dry vermouth
dash Angostura bitters

Stir all the ingredients well
with ice in a pitcher, and
then strain into a chilled
cocktail glass.

Bailey's Comet

The spirit turns the popular creamy liqueur into a rather
stiffer proposition.

1 measure/1½ tbsp vodka
1 measure/1½ tbsp Bailey's

Combine the ingredients with
cracked ice in a rocks glass. The
quantity can safely be doubled
to save time, as you're bound to
want another.

Balalaika

My note on the Czarina applies equally here. The formula is basically a variation on the White Lady recipe, with vodka replacing the gin. As such, it has a slightly milder spirit flavour, but the sharp citrus flavours are still appetizingly apparent.

1¹/₂ measures/6 tsp vodka
³/₄ measure/3 tsp Cointreau
³/₄ measure/3 tsp lemon juice

Shake the ingredients well with plenty of ice, and strain into a cocktail glass. Add an orange-and-cherry garnish.

Black Cossack

You may think its presence will hardly be noticed, but the extra kick given to the beer by the slug of vodka in a Black Cossack is an appreciable one.

1 measure/1¹/₂ tbsp vodka
300ml/¹/₂ pint Guinness

Add well-chilled Guinness to a highball or half-pint glass into which a measure of ice-cold vodka has already been poured. Wait for the head on the beer to settle before drinking.

Sea Breeze

One of today's most requested cocktails, Sea Breeze was one of the first popular cocktails to use cranberry juice. Ocean Spray is one of the most famous brands, but the supermarkets nearly all have a proprietary version.

2 measures/3 tbsp vodka
2 measures/3 tbsp grapefruit juice
3 measures/4¹/₂ tbsp cranberry
*   juice*

Shake all the ingredients well with plenty of ice, and pour everything into a chilled highball glass. Add a wedge of lime and a few cranberries.

Bartending know-how
Cranberry juice is a sugar-and-water product. It is possible to buy apple juice with cranberry if you want neither sugar nor water.

Liberator

Here is another of those cocktails full of blended, tropical fruit flavours, to which a vodka base lends itself so well.

1¹/₂ measures/6 tsp vodka
¹/₂ measure/2 tsp Midori
or other melon liqueur
2 measures/3 tbsp mango juice
¹/₂ measure/2 tsp lime juice

Shake all the ingredients well with ice, and strain into a cocktail glass. Garnish with a neatly cut sliver of mango and a slice of lime.

Camshaft

I am not at all certain how this drink came to be named after part of a car engine. Perhaps the fruit juices in it act as sliding parts to facilitate the passage of the alcohol.

1 measure/1¹/₂ tbsp vodka
¹/₂ measure/2 tsp Campari
1 measure/1¹/₂ tbsp passion
fruit juice
1 measure/1¹/₂ tbsp orange juice
1 measure/1¹/₂ tbsp sparkling
lemonade

Pour the ingredients in this order into a rocks glass half-full of cracked ice. Stir briefly and gently, being careful not to neutralize the fizz in the lemonade. Garnish with a half-slice of orange and a half-slice of lemon.

Hammer Horror

Use the best vanilla ice cream you can find for this, and preferably one that is made with whole egg and real vanilla, for extra richness.

1 measure/1½ tbsp vodka
1 measure/1½ tbsp Kahlúa
60ml/4 tbsp vanilla ice cream

Add all the ingredients to a liquidizer with cracked ice, blend for a few seconds and then strain into a cocktail glass. Sprinkle the surface of the drink with grated dark chocolate.

Kew Punch

This is a drinkable concoction of vodka, sweet vermouth, curaçao, gin and cherry brandy served over fresh summer fruits.

1 measure/1½ tbsp vodka
1 measure/1½ tbsp sweet
  red vermouth
1 measure/1½ tbsp orange curaçao
²/₃ measure/1 tbsp gin
²/₃ measure/1 tbsp cherry brandy
assorted soft summer fruits, sliced
1–2 dashes Angostura bitters
2 measures/3 tbsp American
  dry ginger ale
2 measures/3 tbsp sparkling
  lemonade
1 lemon

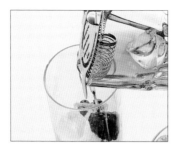

2 Strain into a highball glass full of ice cubes and the sliced summer fruits (peach, apricot, strawberries, raspberries, etc).

3 Add the bitters, and then pour in the chilled ginger ale and lemonade to taste.

4 To make the lemon triangles, pare a thin piece of lemon rind from the lemon.

5 Cut the rind into a rectangle and cut a slit three-quarters of the way across the rind. Turn the rectangle and repeat from the other side.

6 Twist to form a triangle, crossing the ends to secure. Add to the drink with leaves of lemon balm or mint.

1 Measure the vodka, vermouth, curaçao, gin and cherry brandy into a pitcher of ice and stir well to chill.

French Horn

The drink calls for a particular variety of French liqueur called Chambord, made from black raspberries. If you can't find it, substitute ordinary crème de framboise. Its sweetness is thrown into relief with the neutrality of the vodka and the sharpness of the lemon juice.

1 measure/1¹/₂ tbsp vodka
³/₄ measure/3 tsp Chambord
   (or crème de framboise)
¹/₂ measure/2 tsp lemon juice

Stir the ingredients in a pitcher with plenty of ice. Strain into a cocktail glass and garnish with a whole raspberry.

Kir Lethale

The raisins for this cocktail should be soaked overnight in vodka to give the drink that extra kick. This is a party recipe to serve six.

6 vodka-soaked raisins
30ml/2 tbsp vodka
3 measures/4$^1/_2$ tbsp crème
    de cassis
1 bottle brut champagne or dry
    sparkling wine, chilled

Place a vodka-soaked raisin at the bottom of each glass. Add $^1/_4$ measure/1 tsp plain vodka or the vodka from the steeped raisins, if using, to each glass. Add $^1/_2$ measure/2 tsp crème de cassis to each and finish the drinks with the champagne or sparkling wine.

Slow Comfortable Screw

The 1970s idea of a joke in the drink's name may be a touch embarrassing now, but the mixture is a good one, and the drink was something of a modern classic a generation ago. "Slow" refers to the sloe gin, "comfortable" is the Southern Comfort and "screw" is the Screwdriver (vodka and orange).

1 measure/1½ tbsp vodka
¾ measure/3 tsp Southern Comfort
¾ measure/3 tsp sloe gin
5 measures/120ml/4fl oz orange juice

1 Add the first three ingredients to a highball glass half-packed with ice.

2 Stir to combine, and then top up with the orange juice. Garnish with a cocktail cherry on a stick for the essential seventies touch, and add two long straws.

3 A plastic novelty will add that final note of sheer class, as will throwing back three of them and then slow-dancing with somebody ghastly.

Soft Fruit and Ginger Cup

This colourful medley of soft fruits is steeped in vodka and served with an icy blend of sorbet and ginger ale. You will definitely need to use spoons. The recipe serves four, and can be used as a summer dinner-party dessert.

115g/4oz strawberries, hulled
115g/4oz raspberries, hulled
50g/2oz blueberries
15ml/1 tbsp caster (superfine) sugar
4 measures/6 tbsp vodka
600ml/1 pint still ginger ale
4 large scoops orange sorbet
1 measure/1¹/₂ tbsp grenadine

1 Cut the strawberries in half and put them in a bowl with the raspberries, blueberries and sugar. Pour over the vodka and toss lightly. Cover and chill for at least 30 minutes.

2 Put the ginger ale and sorbet in a blender or food processor and process until smooth. Pour into four bowl-shaped glasses and add a couple of ice cubes to each glass.

3 Spoon ¹/₄ measure/1 tsp grenadine over the ice cubes in each glass, then spoon the vodka-steeped fruits on top of the sorbet mixture and ice cubes. Garnish each glass with a physalis and serve.

Vodka and Kumquat Lemonade

This is a mild-sounding name for what is a strong concoction of kumquat and peppercorn-flavoured vodka and white curaçao. The recipe comfortably serves two, in long glasses.

90g/3oz kumquats
5 measures/120ml/4fl oz vodka
3 black peppercorns
²/₃ measure/1 tbsp white curaçao
²/₃ measure/1 tbsp lemon juice
7 measures/150ml/¹/₄ pint
   sparkling mineral or
   soda water
fresh mint leaves

2 Fill a pitcher with cracked ice. Add the curaçao, lemon juice and flavoured vodka with the sliced kumquats (not the peppercorns). Stir well with a long swizzle-stick.

4 Pour the drink into chilled glasses containing ice cubes.

1 Thickly slice the kumquats and add to the vodka in an airtight jar with the cracked black peppercorns. Set aside for at least a couple of hours or overnight if possible.

3 Add the mineral or soda water and a few fresh mint leaves and gently stir everything together.

5 Transfer slices of vodka-soaked kumquats from the pitcher to the glasses and garnish with extra mint sprigs.

Hot Cherry

Solve the Russo-Polish dispute as to which of them originally invented vodka by combining both nationalities (in even-handed measure of course) in this exciting cocktail. The tonic water adds a pleasantly bitter note to the rich cherry fruitiness of the mixture.

1 measure/1¹/₂ tbsp Stolichnaya
   vodka
1 measure/1¹/₂ tbsp Wisniowka
   (Polish cherry vodka)
2 measures/3 tbsp tonic water

Shake the vodkas with plenty of cracked ice, strain into a rocks glass containing two ice cubes and add the tonic. Garnish with a cherry.

Pushkin's Punch

This powerful cocktail is named after the great Russian writer. Use a good sparkling wine from Australia or California.

1 measure/1¹/₂ tbsp vodka
1 measure/1¹/₂ tbsp Grand Marnier
dash lime juice
dash orange bitters (or orange
   curaçao)
dry sparkling wine

Shake the first four ingredients with ice, and strain into a chilled, large wine goblet. Top up with sparkling wine.

Woo Woo

A creation of the 1980s, Woo Woo was one of the first cocktail recipes to use peach schnapps. Archer's Peach County was the brand preferred, and the recipe is still a popular one on today's cocktail lists.

1 measure/1¹/₂ tbsp vodka
1¹/₂ measures/6 tsp peach schnapps
4 measures/6 tbsp cranberry juice

Shake all the ingredients well with ice, and strain into a highball glass half-filled with cracked ice.

Bartending know-how
Peach schnapps is not really a true schnapps, but a sort of schnapps-based liqueur. Archer's now make lime and cranberry versions to supplement the original peach.

Green Dragon

You will find that one glass of this dry, savoury and extremely strong cocktail is more than enough. Sip it slowly, or be brave and take it at a couple of gulps. Then lie down.

2 measures/3 tbsp Stolichnaya vodka
1 measure/1¹/₂ tbsp green Chartreuse

Shake the ingredients well with ice, and strain into a cocktail glass. Garnish with a cocktail onion on a swizzle-stick.

Piranha

This is one of those deceptive cocktails that tastes relatively harmless, but in fact packs quite a bite, much like the predatory flesh-eating fish after which it is named.

1¹/₂ measures/6 tsp vodka
1 measure/1¹/₂ tbsp brown
   crème de cacao
1 measure/1¹/₂ tbsp ice-cold cola

Pour the alcohol into a rocks glass containing plenty of cracked ice and stir vigorously, before adding the cola.

Bartending know-how
Brands of cola have proliferated like wildfire ever since the success of the original Coca-Cola. There are low-sugar and caffeine-free versions, and there is now a French brand aimed at the Muslim market.

Boyar

The name of this vodka cocktail has Russian origins, "boyars" being members of the upper nobility in Russia from the 10th through to the 17th century. This very dry and herb-tinged mixture would make a good appetite-whetter at a party where nibbles are going to be served. The tiny quantity of kümmel shines through, and leaves a very appetizing aftertaste in its wake.

2 measures/3 tbsp vodka
1/2 measure/2 tsp dry vermouth
1/4 measure/1 tsp kümmel

Shake with ice, and strain into a cocktail glass. The drink doesn't need a garnish.

Nevsky Prospekt

The Russian reference here is to a boulevard in Moscow. You can add ¹/₄ measure/1 tsp sugar syrup if you feel it needs a touch of extra sweetness, but I prefer it quite sour.

1¹/₂ measures/6 tsp Stolichnaya vodka
¹/₂ measure/2 tsp light rum
¹/₂ measure/2 tsp orange curaçao
¹/₄ measure/1 tsp lime juice

Shake all the ingredients well with ice, and strain into a cocktail glass. Garnish with a half-slice of lime.

Borodino

Let's get serious. This is a strong cocktail, with the ingredients in the 37.5% to 40% alcohol range, but the result is a virginal-looking white drink.

1 measure/1¹/₂ tbsp vodka
1 measure/1¹/₂ tbsp gin
1 measure/1¹/₂ tbsp Cointreau

Shake all the ingredients well with ice, and strain into a cocktail glass. Add a small piece of orange rind.

Sex on the Beach

A variation on Woo Woo, this version has more fruit juice. The name has, not surprisingly, kept it popular in seaside resorts, as the next best resort after sex.

1 measure/1¹/₂ tbsp vodka
1 measure/1¹/₂ tbsp peach
    schnapps
3 measures/4¹/₂ tbsp cranberry
    juice
3 measures/4¹/₂ tbsp pineapple
    juice

Half-fill a highball glass with cracked ice, add all the ingredients in the above order, and stir vigorously. Garnish with pieces of pineapple and orange.

Blue Shark

Blue curaçao produces a beautiful effect when mixed with clear spirits. This is a popular American drink.

1 measure/1¹/₂ tbsp vodka
1 measure/1¹/₂ tbsp tequila
¹/₂ measure/2 tsp blue curaçao

Shake all the ingredients well with ice, and strain into a small rocks glass. Squeeze a little orange rind over the drink to release the oil, but don't add the rind itself.

SOS

Lemon vodka is called for in this drink. Russian types are termed limonnaya and flavoured with natural lemon essence, or there is a mixed citrus version made by the Swedish Absolut company called Citron.

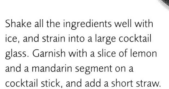

1 measure/1¹/2 tbsp lemon vodka
1 measure/1¹/2 tbsp peach schnapps
2 measures/3 tbsp unsweetened mandarin juice (from a can, if necessary)
¹/4 measure/1 tsp grenadine

Shake all the ingredients well with ice, and strain into a large cocktail glass. Garnish with a slice of lemon and a mandarin segment on a cocktail stick, and add a short straw.

Prussian Salute

This is one of those hardcore cocktails that's all alcohol with no mixers. The sweet fruit notes in it help to soften its impact a little – but not much.

1¹/2 measures/6 tsp vodka
¹/2 measure/2 tsp crème de mûre
¹/2 measure/2 tsp slivovitz
¹/2 measure/2 tsp Cointreau

Shake all the ingredients well with ice, and strain into a cocktail glass. Garnish with a slice of lemon.

Kempinsky Fizz

A luxuriously fruity, fizzy mixture with a delicate pinkish colour, this would kick off a dinner party in fine style.

1¹/₂ measures/6 tsp vodka
¹/₂ measure/2 tsp crème de cassis
¹/₄ measure/1 tsp lemon juice
4 measures/6 tbsp sparkling
* ginger ale*

Half-fill a chilled tall glass with ice, add the first three ingredients, stir briskly and then top up with ginger ale.

Bartending know-how
The original home of syrupy crème de cassis is Burgundy in eastern France, where much is made in Dijon. As a classic fruit liqueur, it dates back to the mid-19th century, and its principal export market today – somewhat surprisingly – is Japan, where they mix it with soda.

Long Island Iced Tea

This is a long, powerful drink with a rumbustiously intoxicating effect, its potency well disguised by the cola. For a simpler version, use equal quantities of rum, Cointreau, tequila and lemon juice, and top up with cola. The recipe does not contain tea. It's a facetious way of referring to the fact that it looks innocuously like a glass of non-alcoholic iced tea.

1/2 measure/2 tsp white rum
1/2 measure/2 tsp vodka
1/2 measure/2 tsp gin
1/2 measure/2 tsp silver tequila
1/2 measure/2 tsp Cointreau
1/2 measure/2 tsp sugar syrup
juice of half a lemon
4 measures/6 tbsp cola

3 Stir well for 30 seconds to chill the mixture.

5 Strain into a highball glass filled with ice cubes and a twist of lemon.

1 Fill a pitcher with cracked ice and add the white rum, vodka, gin, silver tequila and Cointreau.

2 Add the sugar syrup to the spirits in the pitcher.

4 Add lemon juice to taste.

6 Add chilled cola, and finish with a sprig of fresh mint.

Index

DRINK AWARENESS
Always drink legally
and responsibly. Do
not drink and drive,
and avoid alcohol
whilst pregnant or
trying to conceive.

This edition is published by
Lorenz Books, an imprint of
Anness Publishing Ltd,
www.annesspublishing.com;
info@anness.com

A CIP catalogue record for this
book is available from the British
Library.

Publisher: Joanna Lorenz
Senior Editor: Felicity Forster
Photographers: Frank Adam, and
    Steve Baxter
Designer: Nigel Partridge
Production Controller: Ben
    Worley

PUBLISHER'S NOTE
Although the advice and
information in this book are
believed to be accurate and true
at the time of going to press
neither the authors nor the
publisher can accept any legal
responsibility or liability for any
errors or omissions that may have
been made nor for any
inaccuracies nor for any loss,
harm or injury that comes about
from following instructions or
advice in this book.